JU MIPHAM NAMGYAL'S

WAY OF THE REALIZED OLD DOGS

ADVICE THAT POINTS OUT THE ESSENCE OF MIND, CALLED "A LAMP THAT DISPELS DARKNESS"

TONY DUFF

PADMA KARPO TRANSLATION COMMITTEE

This text is secret and should not be shown to those who have not had the necessary introduction and instructions of the Thorough Cut system of Dzogchen meditation. If you have not had the necessary instructions, reading this text can be harmful to your spiritual health! Seal. Seal. Seal.

First edition, February 2009; revised February 2011; second edition October 2012
ISBN Paper: 978-9937-8244-2-2
ISBN E-book: 978-9937-572-51-4

Janson typeface with diacritical marks and
Tibetan Classic typeface
Designed and created by Tony Duff
Tibetan Computer Company
http://www.pktc.org/pktc

Committee members for this book: translation and composition, Lama Tony Duff; editorial, Tom Anderson; cover design, Christopher Duff.

Produced, Printed, and Published by
Padma Karpo Translation Committee
P.O. Box 4957
Kathmandu
NEPAL

Web-site and e-mail contact through:
http://www.tibet.dk/pktc
or search Padma Karpo Translation Committee on the web.

CONTENTS

INTRODUCTION

This book presents the text *The Way of the Realized Old Dogs, Advice that Points out the Essence of Mind, Called "A Lamp that Dispels the Darkness"* by the great Nyingma scholar-practitioner Ju Mipham Namgyal [1846–1912]. Mipham, as he is usually called, has become the most well known of Nyingma scholars. He is so well known these days that no further introduction to him should be needed. His text here concerns the practice of the innermost level of Dzogchen or, in English, Great Completion.

Great Completion

The Dzogchen or Great Completion system of dharma came from a land called Uddiyana, which is thought to have been in what is now the Swat region of Pakistan. In the language of Uddiyana, this system of dharma was called "mahasandhi", meaning exactly "the great juncture". The Tibetans translated this name with "rdzogs pa chen po", which in English means exactly "great completion". In this case, the words "juncture" and "completion" are different but they have the same meaning. They refer to that one all-encompassing space, that one great juncture in which all that there could be—whether enlightened or unenlightened, whether belonging to nirvana or samsara—is complete.

The name Great Completion refers both to an all-inclusive space that beings including humans could realize and to a system of instruction designed to bring beings to the realization of it[1]. When a being does realize it, there is nothing more to be realized or done because all is complete within that being's space of realization and the work of spiritual practice is complete. In a Buddhist way of talking, Great Completion is the final realization in which that being has manifested true and complete buddhahood.

Great Completion has been called "Great Perfection" in English but that presents an incorrect understanding of the name. The final space of realization is not a state of perfection, but one that contains both perfection and imperfection. The name is not intended to connect us with the idea of perfection, but with the idea of the juncture of all things perfect and imperfect, that is, to the idea of a state of realization in which all things are complete.

In relation to this, there is the unavoidable point that Longchen Rabjam's definitive explanations in his revered text *The Dharmadhatu Treasury* make it clear beyond a doubt that the name of the system means "Great Completion" and not "Great Perfection". He mentions in several places that the

---

[1] For realization, see the glossary.

point of the name is the inclusion—just as the original name from Uddiyana states—of all dharmas within a single unique sphere of wisdom.

It is explained within the Great Completion teachings that *Completion* in the name means that all phenomena are included at once in a single space of realization and that *great* is used to distinguish something known by wisdom in direct perception from the same thing known by dualistic mind as a concept. Thus *Great Completion* is not the completion understood through the use of concept, but the greater version of that, the actual state of completion known through wisdom.

Levels of Great Completion Teaching

The Great Completion teaching as a whole consists of many teachings and within them varying levels of profundity can be identified. Early holders of the teachings classified them into three main levels of profundity, with each level being called a section. The three main sections identified were named Mind, Space, and Foremost Instruction sections. Of them, the Foremost Instruction Section contains the most profound teachings of Great Completion. This section was also further divided into levels of increasing profundity of which the most profound level is called by several names such as "nyingthig" meaning "quintessential", "unsurpassed" meaning the most profound explanation, and "innermost" meaning that there is no more subtle level. This quintessential, unsurpassed, innermost level contains the most essential teaching of Great Completion—of reality—that has appeared in our current era of human society. This quintessential teaching consists of two main sections of practice, one called Thorough Cut and one called Direct Crossing.

Mipham's text instructs at the quintessence level and concerns itself with the practice of Thorough Cut but not the practice of Direct Crossing.

Foremost Instructions

Many types of oral instruction are used in order to transmit the Buddhist teachings. Each has a style of its own and each is named accordingly. Unfortunately, the names of the various types of oral instruction have never been translated into English consistently or even correctly, and this has led to a major loss of meaning in the translations. For example, of these different types of oral instruction, there is one that is a key to understanding Quintessential Great Completion. It is the type of oral instruction called "upadesha" in the Sanskrit language. "Desha" means "verbal instruction", simple as that. "Upa" means the one above the others, the one that is better in every way, the one that comes at the front of all other types of instruction. This name was translated into the Tibetan language with "man ngag", where *ngag* means verbal instruction and *man* means the one that comes before all others. In English it is exactly *foremost instruction*.

The particular quality of a foremost type of instruction is that it goes right to the heart of the person being instructed and connects the person very directly to the meaning being presented. It is not just a "pith" or "key" or "oral" instruction as so often translated, but specifically is the foremost of all types of instruction, the one that has the ability to get right into and move the mind of the person who is being instructed.

As mentioned above, the Great Completion teaching can be divided into levels of instruction. The early Indian masters following Garab Dorje—Manjushrimitra, Shri Singha, and others of their time—mostly divided it into the three, successively more profound sections of teaching mentioned just above. The Foremost Instruction Section is named for the fact that its key characteristic is that the instructions at this very profound level of teaching are imparted not with just any oral, pith, key, or what-have-you instruction, but specifically with the *foremost* type of oral *instruction*.

Mipham's text instructs at the Foremost Instruction level of the Great Completion teachings.

Reading Mipham's Text

Mipham's text lays out its subject clearly, with an economy of words, and with very little philosophical talk attached. The reason for this is that he wrote it specifically for the village tantrikas[2] who, in Tibet at least, tended not to have much learning in these subjects. In modern times, we would say that he wrote it specifically for the city-dwelling tantrikas. Another way to say this is that he did not write the text for the learned monks of the monasteries or the knowledgeable tan-

---

[2] "Tantrikas" is the Indian name for followers of the tantric teachings. It was translated into Tibetan with "ngag pa".

trikas living in the retreat centres; if he had done that, the text would be much longer and would use a significantly more technical language than it does. Mipham wrote it to be straightforward enough that the average yogis living in towns and villages, most of whom did not have much learning but who did know the basic points of Great Completion practice, could easily understand the text and use it as a manual for practice.

Mipham wrote the text so well that it soon became a favourite amongst Nyingma practitioners. It became so well known that several, long commentaries were written to explain it in detail. These commentaries also have become very popular because they, like Mipham's original text, focus on explaining the practice of Thorough Cut in a way that is accessible to all tantrikas.

Three commentaries that should be of special interest are very recent ones by Tibetans who, at the very end of the twentieth century, were regarded as the most learned of Great Completion gurus in East Tibet. The three commentaries are a shorter guide and a very extensive commentary both written by Khenpo Jigmey Phuntshog of Serta, and a very extensive set of notes by Ontrul Tenpa'i Wangchuk. Khenpo Jigmey Phuntshog died around the end of the twentieth century, having become well-known around the world. Ontrul Tenpa'i Wangchuk is alive at the time of writing and is very famous within East Tibet.

Ontrul Tenpa'i Wangchuk is a direct disciple of the recent mahasiddha of Dzogchen Monastery, Abu Losang Gyatso, and is regarded as the greatest Quintessence or Nyingthig scholar now living. His extensive notes to Mipham's text are called, *Notes to The Way of the Realized Old Dogs That Points out the Essence of Mind*. I used his notes several times to clarify ambiguous wordings in Mipham's text and on each occasion made a note in order to emphasize to readers that the Great Completion teaching is alive and well in Tibet at the time of writing, even if it is a rather endangered species. Ideally, this book would include a translation of one of the three commentaries mentioned above or of any of several others that have been written and are well-known in the Tibetan system. However, the commentaries are large and their inclusion would delay the publication of this important text.

You can get a clear sense of the meaning of Mipham's text by reading his opening verse, in which he states that he wrote this text for the city-dwelling tantrikas—people who attend to their daily lives with families, and so on, rather than staying in large institutions doing a lot of study. He says that, despite their relative lack of knowledge, the majority of city-dwelling tantrikas can gain significant levels of attainment without much hardship by following the foremost instructions that he will provide. It is so because of the power of this profound path of Quintessential Great Completion.

Moreover, in the colophon, he says that he has written his text in simple dharma language, specifically so that city-dwelling tantrikas will be able to understand it. He also mentions that this is what is called "a heart's blood type of instruction", a term used to indicate the type of instruction where the teacher really lays out the core of something based on his own experience of it.

Although he says that the text is written in easy-to-under-stand dharma language that gets right to the point, he still makes extensive use of the unique and technical terminology of Thorough Cut. This terminology will be hard for many to understand, so I have provided copious notes and an extensive glossary to make it accessible. Additionally, the text in Ti-betan script has been included for the sake of those who are intent upon study and practise of the text.

Despite Mipham's intent to write an easy-to-understand text, it is, like most Tibetan texts, not intended to be understood simply by reading the words. This needs to be said because, in the West especially, in modern times when there is a strong emphasis on education of the rational mind, there is a strong cultural habit of thinking that one should be able to pick up a book and read it and comprehend it. While it is true that this text was written so that an uneducated person could understand the content, the practice discussed in the text can only be known through oral instructions received from a qualified teacher with a lineage.

Differentiations: A Feature of the Text

Although Mipham's purpose in writing his text was to lay out the practice of Thorough Cut in a way that could easily be understood by those without detailed knowledge of the Great Completion teachings, he did include an explanation of the advanced topic within Thorough Cut called "differentia-tions". This is fortunate for us because the instructions on differentiations, though an important part of the Thorough Cut teaching, are not usually recorded in writing but are conveyed only through oral instruction. Therefore, Mipham's explanation of differentiations becomes a special feature of this text and makes it of special interest to all Great Completion practitioners.

There are many differentiations that can be made in the context of the Thorough Cut. Mipham uses one of them in this text in order to introduce the dharmakaya in an easy-to-understand way. It shows the difference between alaya, as a part of dualistic mind, and dharmakaya, which is wisdom. The Thorough Cut teaching talks about various types of alaya and talks about alaya in various ways. The variety and differences can be quite confusing, even for someone with some technical knowledge. Because of this, Mipham's discussion of the ala`ya will need clarification for most readers. One value of the commentaries to Mipham's text mentioned earlier is that they spend time on making such a clarification. Note for the moment that alaya and alaya consciousness are two different things.

To help overcome these two issues of paucity of written teaching on differentiation and a need for clarification of alaya, I have translated a short but very clear text that lays out several differentiations and which clearly distinguishes between some of the different types of alaya. The book is called *Differentiating Non-Distraction and So Forth*[3].

---

[3] By Tony Duff and published by Padma Karpo Translation Committee, 2008. ISBN: 978-9937-9031-2-7.

Further Study

Padma Karpo Translation Committee has amassed a range of materials to help those who are studying this and related topics. Please see the chapter Supports for Study at the end of the book for the details.

Health Warning

The text here is about a subject that is kept secret. Anyone who has had these teachings in person will be able to understand them or at least go to his teacher and ask for further explanation. Anyone who has had the introduction to the nature of mind[4] upon which the teachings hinge, please use and enjoy the text as you will! However, if you have not heard these teachings and especially if you have not had a proper introduction to the nature of your mind, you would be better off not reading this book but seeking out someone who could teach it to you. Nowadays there are both non-Tibetans and Tibetans who can do that for you and who are available in many countries across our planet. In short, the contents of this book could be dangerous to your spiritual health if you are not ready for it, so exercise care.

These days, in the times of rampant globalization, these deep secrets have become very public. That is not necessarily a good thing. For example, I have many times in the last few years run into young men who are extremely confident of

---

[4] For introduction, see the glossary.

their understanding of the meaning of these profound systems but who just spout words that they have read in books. Unfortunately, they have read the books and know the words but have not contacted the inner meaning that the books are intended merely as a pointer towards. The solidity of their minds is noticeable and is not being helped by reading these things for which they are not ready and, therefore, should not be reading.

My best wishes to all of you.
May you preserve the state!

Tony Duff
Padma Karpo Translation Committee
Swayambhunath,
Nepal,
October, 2012

THE WAY OF THE REALIZED OLD DOGS, ADVICE THAT POINTS OUT THE ESSENCE OF MIND, CALLED "A LAMP THAT DISPELS THE DARKNESS"

by Ju Mipham Namgyal

I prostrate to the guru and to the Manjushri Wisdom Being[5].

> Without need of vast training in hearing and
>   contemplating
> A majority of village tantrikas who preserve the
>   essence of mind will,
> Using the way of foremost instruction, go with little
>   hardship
> To the level of the vidyadharas because it has the
>   power of a profound path.

Now, to talk about that here, you set this mind of yours in its untouched condition, without any involvement in thought at all and then, in that state, you preserve[6] a continuous stream

---

[5] Skt. mañjuśhrī jñānasatva. Manjushri Wisdom Being is a name for the superfactual form of Manjushri.

[6] For preserve, see the glossary.

of mindfulness. This will cause an even[7], indeterminate[8] awareness[9] that is dark and oblivious[10] to occur. When, within that, there is no production at all of vipashyana[11] which knows this and that, then, due to that particular aspect of it, the gurus designate it as "ignorance". And, due to the particular aspect of not being able to say what it is like because there is no identification of it as being like so and so or such and such, they designate it as "indeterminate"[12]. And, not being able to say where it was abiding or what it was thinking, they call it "ordinary evenness"[13]. That is how it is, and to be that way is to be in the state of the ordinary type of alaya[14].

---

[7] Tib. btang snyoms. He glosses "even" just below.

[8] Tib. lung ma bstan. He glosses "indeterminate" just below.

[9] For awareness, see the glossary.

[10] Tib. thom me ba. "Oblivious" means a sort of blanked-out state in which you lose track of what is happening in mind.

[11] For vipashyana, see the glossary.

[12] This explains the wording "indeterminate" just applied to this state.

[13] When it says ordinary, it means nothing special, just the ordinary type of even-ness meaning even-placement of mind, that samsaric beings have or can develop. "Even" means a state that is not this and not that, which explains the first mention, just above, of this word where it was used to refer to such a state.

[14] "Ordinary" has the same meaning as just given above. In this case it means ordinary old alaya, just as it is for an ordinary samsaric person, and without any consideration of higher realities that might be contained within that alaya.

That type of placement of mind[15] has to be used in order to arouse wisdom[16] but, given that it does not have wisdom knowing its own face shining forth[17] within it, it is not the main meditation; as the *Samanta Prayer[18]* says,

> The oblivion of no thought process at all ꣼
> Itself is ignorance, the cause of confusion ... ꣼

That sort of oblivious awareness in which there is no thought process and no movement is experienced by mind. Therefore, that one which is aware of the fact of that, that is, that one which is just sitting there without doing any thinking, looks from its own situation at itself[19] and if, by doing so, a rigpa[20] arises that is free of movement and thought process, that is fully visible[21] yet without out and in[22] like a clear sky,

---

[15] For mind, see the glossary.

[16] For wisdom, see the glossary.

[17] For shining forth, see the glossary.

[18] The Prayer of Samantabhadra which can be found within the *Mind of Samantabhadra Fully Visible Tantra*. This is a very popular prayer amongst Great Completion practitioners. Translations of it into English have been published.

[19] Ontrul Tenpa'i Wangchuk's *Notes* indicates that this means that the awareness that exists in that unthinking state of oblivion stays in its own place and looks right at its own innate character.

[20] Rigpa in general means a dynamic type of knowing, one that sees what is going on. See the glossary for more.

[21] Fully visible has the same meaning as transparency for which

(continued...)

that is without the duality of something to be experienced and an experiencer of it, yet which, of itself, firmly decides on its own nature so thinks, "There is nothing other than this", then, given that it is something about which there is no way, using thoughts or expressions, to say, "It is like this", it could be designated "divorced from extremes[23]", "beyond expression[24]", "the innate situation's luminosity", and "rigpa"[25]. That is so because self-introducing wisdom has shone forth and by doing so the darkness of the oblivion of blindness has been cleared off; like the sun's rising has let you see the inside of your house so, with this, a certainty about the reality of your own mind has been produced. This is called "the foremost instruction connected with cracking open the eggshell of ignorance".

---

[21](...continued)
see the glossary.

[22] In other words, one which knows, but not as something in here knowing something out there.

[23] Extremes are concepts; because they are not the actual situation they either overstate or understate it.

[24] "Expression" means any mental or verbal expression made using concepts.

[25] Here rigpa has the specific sense of the rigpa met with on the path of Great Completion.

When that sort of realization[26] happens, because the reality that goes with it is the primordially-present nature being what it is, there is the understanding that it is not compounded by cause and condition and is without shift or change into the three times[27]. With this, there is no observance of the existence of even an atom of what could be called "mind which is other than this"[28].

The darkness of oblivion that came prior to this was not expressible, but that was a case of not being able to express it because of not knowing what it was and so not being able to identify it to begin with. The face of rigpa also is not expressible, but this is a case of a fact that is simply inexpressible known with a doubt-free decision about what it is. Thus, there is a great difference between the inexpressibility of these two, similar to the difference between not having and having

---

[26] In Great Completion and Mahamudra, the particular event of recognizing your innate wisdom mind through what is called "rigpa", is called "realization". "Realization" here has that meaning and refers to that event which has just happened. For realization, see the glossary.

[27] Without shift or change into the three times means that it never changes into the samsaric type of mind which itself is the situation in which the three times are present.

[28] In other words, this is it, this is the nature of your own mind that has been primordially present just as it is in its own way of being. Seeing that, which is the meaning here of "realization", you understand that it is not like samsaric mind and, at the same time, you do not see the tiniest amount of any other kind of mind than just this.

eyes respectively, and, with that, the distinction between alaya and dharmakaya is included in this point, too.

Following on from that, what is referred to with "common awareness"[29], "no mentation", "beyond expression", and so on has both authentic and non-authentic sides. Therefore, if you ascertain the key point of noble meaning within same-sounding terminology, you will discover the experiences of the mind of profound dharma[30].

In regard to this putting oneself untouched into the state of mind's essence, one faction claims that what is to be done is to preserve mere illumination, mere knowing, then to set oneself in a state that has the thought, "It is illumination coming from mental consciousness"[31]. Another faction claims

---

[29] For common awareness, see the glossary.

[30] All the names given are special names for the special experience of rigpa but also are used for ordinary, samsaric states of mind. Thus, the words themselves have two referents—the authentic or nirvanic side and the non-authentic or samsaric side. In the practice of Thorough Cut (and also in Essence Mahamudra), current experience that could be described with these terms has to be assessed to see whether it is the noble—meaning gone beyond samsaric experience—side or not. Making this kind of differentiation between the two possibilities is the path that leads to the direct experience of the special possibility of profound dharma.

[31] The definition of consciousness is that it is "illuminative and knowing". These words could apply to samsaric consciousness and states of mind as much as they could to nirvanic wisdom. One group is mistakenly saying that the experience of ordinary,
(continued...)

that it is a mental stabilization in which mind is fixed onto an emptied-out sort of experience that comes from a flat emptiness type of awareness[32]. However, both of these are mere clinging to experience involved with mental consciousness, within grasped-grasping[33]. Therefore, at the time that these are occurring, in the situations of the illumination and the awareness apprehending it and of the emptiness and the awareness apprehending it, the ongoing mindstream which has the apprehending thought process looks at what it is and if, by doing so, the stake of consciousness that has been clinging to the grasped-grasping is uprooted and a decision concerning a naked, starkly-evident situation of a luminous emptiness that is free from centre and fringe arises, that is named "the face of rigpa". In other words, if a crystal clearness arises, that is named "the face of rigpa". It is rigpa free from the outer coverings of the experiences of grasping—in other words, naked wisdom—shining forth. This is called,

---

[31](...continued)
mental consciousness, because it has these qualities like the ones of rigpa, is the rigpa of Thorough Cut. Having made that mistake, the state into which they set themselves is actually mental consciousness thinking that it is the luminosity of rigpa. A particular one of the four schools of Tibetan Buddhism is known for this mistake but Mipham, and I in accord with him, politely leave out the name of the school.

[32] Another mistake that can be made is to go to a state which emphasizes emptiness but which is still within dualistic consciousness. A flat emptiness is a wide open, even state but with nothing happening. That sort of abiding has lost the luminosity aspect, somewhat. Again, one school commonly makes this mistake.

[33] For grasped-grasping, see the glossary.

"The foremost instruction connected with cutting the net of becoming[34]".

Similarly, rigpa divorced from its various outer coverings of experiences connected with mental analysis, like with a grain of wheat and its husks and hairs, has to be identified via reality's own condition illuminating itself[35]. Simply to recognize rigpa's actual condition is not sufficient. Following that, there has to be within just that state of recognition, a practise of familiarization[36] which has a steady abiding with it. An undistracted preservation of a continuity of mindfulness in relation to such an awareness that has been put set into its own condition is important[37].

---

[34] For becoming, see the glossary.

[35] Similar to what was said in the last paragraph, there is a process that has to be followed. The actual wheat grain is inside the ear of wheat with its hairs and husks. The wheat inside the outer covering is what decides on its being wheat just as the inner reality of mind, what it is exactly, decides on what mind actually is.

[36] The word "meditation" is avoided in this type of instruction because (the actual word Tib, "sgom" for) "meditation" implies creation of something that did not previously exist and cultivation of that in order to create something new. In this case, there is nothing to be created but one does have to become increasingly familiar with what is already there.

[37] The type of mindfulness is not the ordinary mindfulness of samsaric mind, it is the dharmata mindfulness that, without conceived effort, keeps the experience of the recognized rigpa in place.

When preserving like that[38], at times there will be a stupefied no-thought in which there is no knowing what it is, at times a full visibility no-thought which has the pure portion of vipashyana turned out[39], at times clinging to temporary experiences of bliss, at times no clinging to temporary experiences of bliss, at times temporary experiences of clarity of this and that with grasping, at times pure, unpolluted clarity separated from grasping, at times rough temporary experiences that are not nice, at times smooth temporary experiences that are delightful, at times loss of meditation because of following after greater levels of disturbance that come from greater levels of discursive thought, at times a polluted state that comes from unabating thickness, and so on. Such waves of thought—to which we have habituated ourselves since beginningless time—and waves of karmic winds will arise in various ways that are uncertain in nature and un-assessable in extent[40]. When you have been on this kind of path for a long time, if there are events like seeing situations filled with strife and dissension, do not approach them with grasping that goes

---

[38] Now he has moved on to discussing the temporary experiences that occur during the course of the practice. The three main ones are bliss, clarity, and no-thought; see the entry in the glossary. They can come in either of two ways. After that, there are many other possibilities.

[39] This item is the recognized rigpa. "Full visibility" means the same as transparency, for which see the glossary.

[40] Ontrul Tenpa'i Wangchuk's *Notes* says: "They will come on in various ways, some of them that are expected and some not; altogether, you cannot know exactly how much or how they will come".

with trying to make them turn out a certain way[41], rather, keep on with your own path. Especially, when you are not doing the familiarization, various discursive thoughts can blaze up like a fire, bringing disturbance; when that happens, do not let them stop you. Keeping a balance between tightness and looseness, maintain your course and then, through that, the experiences of attainment, and so on, that come later will gradually arise.[42]

At this time, generally speaking, the differences between rigpa and not rigpa[43], alaya and dharmakaya, consciousness and wisdom will be an issue. The guru introduces you to these using

---

[41] Ontrul Tenpa'i Wangchuk's *Notes* says that, because of our habits of thinking and karma, all sorts of bad things can start to happen as we proceed on the path. However, there is no fast fix for these things. We have to leave them be, without the kind of grasping that would have things be otherwise, and keep working on the path, a step at a time. One day, we will get the fruit.

[42] This paragraph is about the temporary experiences that inevitably arise on the path. He lays many of them out. In particular, he says that the bad ones do happen as the path goes on. He says not to get involved with attempting to change them but to get on with the work of practising the path. Especially, when really strong ones happen, do not allow them to take you away from the path, instead, keeping a balance, continue with your work. Eventually these kinds of experiences will give way to the later experiences of the path that go with the various levels of attainment.

[43] Tib. ma rig pa. This term is usually translated as "ignorance" but in fact is "not rigpa", the opposite of "rigpa". Here, it has to be translated as "not rigpa" or the point is lost.

foremost instructions which are based on his experience, so that you can gain assurance[44] about them.[45]

Having gained that assurance, when you are preserving, you have to make use of the foremost instruction which states that consciousness left to be itself will have its reality, wisdom, automatically become evident, automatically come to the fore, in the same way as water left undisturbed will become pure. It is not that you try to improve the withdrawal and proliferation[46] that goes with the intellectual understanding found in books and within the arena of investigating what to adopt and to reject with thoughts like, "Is this meditation of

---

[44] Tib. gdeng. "Assurance" is not "certainty". A man might be certain that he can fly but a bird, because it knows it has wings and actually can do so, has the assurance of flying. Here, because you are introduced in direct perception to these things by the guru who gives you foremost instructions based on his experience, you do not merely gain certainty but gain assurance. This is not beginner's talk, this is talk for people who have been on the path for some time.

[45] This is where he makes the differentiation between alaya and dharmakaya.

[46] "Withdrawal and proliferation" are the two sides of thinking. Your mind starts to think and, having thought, reels itself back in from the thought. Then it starts again. When you train intellect well, it becomes very efficient and capable at proliferating and then withdrawing back in from the thought process.

mine consciousness or wisdom?"; that sort of thing will cause both shamatha and vipashyana to become a little obscured[47].

If you manage to develop a steady familiarization which has the style of a naturally-occurring connection between a shamatha that is a steady stream of mindfulness over a placement within own condition and a vipashyana that is one's own face self-illuminated, then the shamatha-vipashyana in which there is primordial inseparability of primordial abiding in own condition and the nature luminosity[48], that is, in which there is self-arising wisdom, the actual mind of Great Completion, will shine forth. This is called "the foremost instruction connected with abiding in equality[49] like space".

Glorious Saraha also spoke in the same way, when he said,

---

[47] Anything based on development within dualistic mind will have the qualities of concentrating and then moving off into elaboration of thought. The usual approach within that framework is to attempt improvement. However, the meaning of being within non-dualistic mind is not that approach at all. It is beyond books and conceptual ways of thought. Analysing whether you are in rigpa or not or dharmakaya or not or wisdom or not is not what is to be done.

[48] "The primordial abiding in its own condition" is the self-existing shamatha of rigpa and "the nature, luminosity" is the self-existing vipashyana of rigpa. The two are primordially unified. That itself is rigpa, self-arising wisdom ...

[49] Tib. mnyam pa nyid. "Equality" is a name for emptiness in this system given that it causes all phenomena to be experienced as equal.

> Thought and to be thought of are utterly
>   abandoned, then in that
> One is to abide without thought in the way that a
>   small child does ...

which is about the method for placement. Then he said,

> If, holding firmly to the guru's authoritative words,
>   you make supreme effort ...

He followed that by stating the conclusion which is that, when you have received the foremost instruction introducing you to rigpa,

> There is no doubt that co-emergence will occur.

In other words, from the very outset your own mind has been happening together with co-emergence mind's reality—rigpa self-arising wisdom—and that is not different from the reality of all dharmas either; it is what is innate to you, the factual luminosity.[50]

So, this approach of putting mind into its own condition then preserving the rigpa that is now recognizing its own face or, you could also say, preserving the essence or reality of mind that has been made manifest, is the foremost instruction that

---

[50] What Mipham has done here is tie the Essence Mahamudra instructions of Saraha to the Thorough Cut instructions of Great Completion instructions of his system. One implication is that they both are saying the same thing. The four lines given are a verse that is frequently quoted in the Kagyu Mahamudra lineage as showing the whole path of Mahamudra.

draws together one hundred key points. To do "continuous preservation" is the same.[51]

The measure of familiarization is known through nighttime luminosity. The sign of its being the path of the authentic is that there is realization occurring through a natural increase of faith, compassion, prajna, and so on; being happy and having few problems is something that comes with having one's own, personal experience of this. This path's profundity and swiftness are known through comparison with the extent of realization attained and the amount of exertion required for it by those who engage in paths other than this.[52]

By meditating on your own mind of luminosity, you will gain the fruition. Or, you could say, discursive thoughts appearing on your own mind of luminosity and its obscurations of latencies will self-cleanse and, while that is happening, the two knowledges will be blossoming without conceived effort and, when that has happened, the primordial seat of power

---

[51] In other words, this is the one foremost instruction that is the very core key point. There are hundreds of foremost instructions but if you distill their real meaning into one instruction, this one is it. It comes right down to recognizing and then doing nothing but continuously preserving it.

[52] Generally, this path is said to be the most profound and the most rapid. However, for a very good presentation of the details of how this path compares to other paths of the higher tantras, see the book *About the Three Lines that Strike Key Points* by Tony Duff, published by Padma Karpo Translation Committee, ISBN: 978-9937-8244-4-6, which presents a text of Dodrupchen III.

will be assumed and the three kayas will be spontaneously existing for you[53].

Profound! Secret! Samaya!

On the twelfth day of the second month of the fire horse year, for the village tantrikas and others like them who do not make great efforts at hearing and contemplating but who want to practice the essence of mind, I, Mipham Jampal Dorje, wrote this profound advice using easy-to-understand dharma language in the form of a heart's blood instruction that shows the experiences of the realized old dogs in general. Goodness. Mangalam.

---

[53] He makes a play on the Tibetan word for "buddha" within this sentence which cannot be directly translated into English. Basically, he says that your mind will self-cleanse, where "cleanse" is the first part of the Tibetan word for buddha, and then that your two knowledges will blossom, where "blossom" is the second part of the Tibetan word for buddha. In short, he is saying that, if you practise this method of the essence of mind, you will become a buddha in a naturally-occurring process that ends with the attainment of the spontaneously-existing three kayas of a buddha. It is very elegant!

GLOSSARY

Alaya, Skt. ālaya, Tib. kun gzhi: This term, if translated, is usually translated as all-base or thereabouts. It is a Sanskrit term that means a range that underlies and forms a basis for something else. In Buddhist teaching, it means a particular level of mind that sits beneath all other levels of mind. However, it is used in several different ways in the Buddhist teaching and changes to a different meaning in each case. In the Great Completion teachings, an important distinction is made between ālaya alone and ālaya consciousness.

Alertness, Tib. shes bzhin: Alertness is a specific mental event that occurs in dualistic mind. It and another mental event, mindfulness, are the two functions of mind that must be developed in order to develop shamatha or one-pointedness of mind. In that context, mindfulness is what remembers the object of the concentration and holds the mind to it while alertness is the mind watching the situation to ensure that the mindfulness is not lost. If distraction does occur, alertness will know it and will inform the mind to re-establish mindfulness again.

Alteration, altered: Same as contrivance *q.v.*

Assurance, Tib. gdeng: Although often translated as confidence, this term means assurance with all of the extra meaning conveyed by that term. A bird might be confident of its ability to fly but more than that, it has the assurance that it will not fall to the ground because of knowing that it has wings and the training to use them. Similarly, a person might be confident that he could liberate the afflictions but not be assured of doing so because of lack of training or other causes. However, a person who has accumulated the causes to be able to liberate afflictions is assured of the ability to do so.

Awareness, Skt. jñā, Tib. shes pa. "Awareness" is always used in our translations to mean the basic knower of mind or, as Buddhist teaching itself defines it, "a general term for any registering mind", whether dualistic or non-dualistic. Hence, it is used for both samsaric and nirvanic situations; for example, consciousness (Tib. "rnam par shes pa") is a dualistic form of awareness, whereas rigpa, wisdom (Tib. "ye shes"), and so on are non-dualistic forms of awareness. See rigpa in the glossary for more.

It is noteworthy that the key term "rigpa" is often mistakenly translated as "awareness", even though it is not merely an awareness; this creates considerable confusion amongst practitioners of the higher tantras who are misled by it.

Becoming, Skt. bhāvanā, Tib. srid pa: This is another name for samsaric existence. Beings in saṃsāra have a samsaric existence but, more than that, they are constantly in a state of becoming—becoming this type of being or that type of being in this abode or that, as they are driven along without choice by the karmic process that drives samsaric existence.

Bliss: Skt. sukha, Tib. bde: The Sanskrit term and its Tibetan translation are usually translated as "bliss" but in fact refer to the whole range of possibilities of everything on the side of good as opposed to bad. Thus, the term will mean pleasant, happy, good, nice, easy, comfortable, blissful, and so on, depending on context.

Bliss, clarity, and no-thought, Tib. bde gsal mi rtog pa: A person who actually practises meditation will have signs of that practice appear as various types of temporary experience. Most commonly, three types of experience are met with: bliss, clarity, and no-thought. Bliss is an ease of body or mind or both, clarity is heightened knowing of mind, and no-thought is an absence of thought that happens in the mind. The three are usually mentioned when discussing the passing experiences that arise because of practising meditation, but there is also a way of describing them as final experiences of realization.

Clarity or Illumination, Skt. vara, Tib. gsal ba: This term should be understood as an abbreviation of the Tibetan term, " 'od gsal ba", meaning luminosity *q.v.* Clarity is not another factor of mind distinct from luminosity, but merely a convenient abbreviation in both Indian and Tibetan dharma language for luminosity.

Clarity, purity, and stability, Tib. gsal dag brten: This is one of the principal instructions for the practise of development stage. It refers to having complete clarity of visualization, complete purity (knowledge of each aspect of the deity's form being a symbol of the complete purity of enlightenment), and stability of the visualization.

Clinging, Tib. zhen pa: In Buddhism, this term refers specifically to the twofold process of dualistic mind mis-taking things that are not true, not pure, as true, pure, etcetera and then, because of seeing them as highly desirable even though they are not, attaching itself to or clinging to those things. This type of clinging acts as a kind of glue that keeps a person joined to the unsatisfactory things of cyclic existence because of mistakenly seeing them as desirable.

Common awareness, Tib. tha mal gyi shes pa: One of several path terms used to indicate mind's essence. It is equivalent to "mindness" and "rigpa". These terms are used by practitioners as a code word for their own, personal experience of the essence of mind. These words are secret because of the power they are connected with and should be kept that way.

This term is often referred to as "ordinary mind", a term that was established by Chogyam Trungpa Rinpoche for his students. However, there are two problems with that word. Firstly, "tha mal" does not mean "ordinary". It means the awareness which is common to all parts of samsaric mind and also which is common to all beings. It is glossed in writings on Mahāmudrā to mean "nature". In other words, it refers to that part of mind which, being common to all events of mind, is its nature. This is well attested to in the writings of the Kagyu forefathers. Secondly, this is not "mind", given that mind is used to mean the dualistic mind of beings in cyclic existence. Rather this is "shes pa", the most general term for all kinds of awareness.

Conceived effort, Tib. rtsol ba: In Buddhism, this term usually does not merely mean effort but has the specific connotation of effort of dualistic mind. In that case, it is effort that is produced by and functions specifically within the context of dualistic concept. For example, the term "mindfulness with effort" specifically means "a type of mindfulness that is occurring within the context of dualistic mind and its various operations". The term "effortless" is often used in Mahāmudrā and Great Completion to mean a way of being in which dualistic mind has been abandoned and, therefore, in which there is none of the striving of ordinary people.

Confusion, Tib. 'khrul pa: In Buddhism, this term mostly refers to the fundamental confusion of taking things the wrong way that happens because of fundamental ignorance, although it can also have the more general meaning of having lots of thoughts and being confused about it. In the first case, it is defined like this "Confusion is the appearance to rational mind of something being present when it is not" and refers, for example, to seeing an object, such as a table, as being truly present, when in fact it is present only as mere, interdependent appearance.

Cyclic existence: See under saṃsāra.

Dharmakaya, Skt. dharmakāya, Tib. chos sku: In the general teachings of Buddhism, this refers to the mind of a buddha, with "dharma" meaning reality and "kāya" meaning body. In the Thorough Cut practice of Great Completion it additionally has the special meaning of being the means by which one rapidly imposes liberation on oneself.

Dharmata, Skt. dharmatā, Tib. chos nyid: This is a general term meaning the way that something is, and can be applied to anything at all; it is similar in meaning to "actuality" *q.v.* For example, the dharmatā of water is wetness and the dharmatā of the becoming bardo is that it is a place where beings are in a samsaric, or becoming mode, prior to entering a nature bardo. It is used frequently in Tibetan Buddhism to mean "the dharmatā of reality", but that is a specific case of the much larger meaning of the term. To read texts which use this term successfully, one has to understand that the term has a general meaning and then see how that applies in context.

Direct Crossing, Tib. thod rgal: The name of one of the two main practices of the innermost level of Great Completion. The other one is Thorough Cut *q.v.*

Discursive thought, Skt. vikalpa, Tib. rnam rtog: This means more than just the superficial thought that is heard as a voice in the head. It includes the entirety of conceptual process that arises due to mind contacting any object of any of the senses. The Sanskrit and Tibetan literally mean "(dualistic) thought (that arises from the mind wandering among the) various superficies *q.v.* (perceived in the doors of the senses)".

Effort, Conceptual effort, Tib. rtsol ba: See under conceived effort.

Entity, Tib. ngo bo: The entity of something is just exactly what that thing is. In English we would often simply say "thing" rather than entity. However, in Buddhism, "thing" has a very specific meaning rather than the general meaning that it has in English. It has become common to translate this term as "essence". However, in most cases "entity", meaning what a thing is rather than an essence of that thing, is the correct translation for this term.

Equipoise and post-attainment, Tib. mnyam bzhag and rjes thob: Although often called "meditation and post-meditation", the actual term is "equipoise and post-attainment". There is great meaning in the actual wording which is lost by the looser translation.

Essence, Tib. ngo bo: This is a key term used throughout Buddhist theory. The original in Sanskrit and the term in Tibetan, too, has both meanings of "essence" and "entity". In some situations the term has more the first meaning and in others, the second. For example, when speaking of mind and mind's essence, it is referring to the core or essential part within mind. On the other hand, when speaking of something such as fire, one can speak of the entity, fire, and its characteristics, such as heat, and so on; in this case, the term does not mean essence but means that thing, what it actually is. See also under entity.

Foremost instruction, Skt. upadeśa, Tib. man ngag: There are several types of instruction mentioned in Buddhist literature: there is the general level of instruction which is the meaning contained in the words of the texts of the tradition; on a more personal and direct level there is oral instruction which has been passed down from teacher to student from the time of the buddha; and on the most profound level there are foremost instructions which are not only oral instructions provided by one's guru but are special, core instructions that come out of personal experience and which convey the teaching concisely and with the full weight of personal experience. Foremost instructions or upadeśha are crucial to the Vajra Vehicle because these are the special way of passing on the profound instructions needed for the student's realization.

Grasped-grasping, Tib. gzung 'dzin: When mind is turned outwardly as it is in the normal operation of dualistic mind, it has developed two faces that appear simultaneously. Special names are given to these two faces: mind appearing in the form of the external object being referenced is called "that which is grasped" and mind appearing in the form of the consciousness that is registering it is called the "grasper" or "grasping" of it. Thus, there is the pair of terms "grasped-grasper" or "grasped-grasping". When these two terms are used, it alerts one to the fact that a Mind Only style of presentation is being discussed. This pair of terms pervades Mind Only, Middle Way, and tantric writings and is exceptionally important in all of them.

Note that one could substitute the word "apprehended" for "grasped" and "apprehender" for "grasper" or "grasping" and that would reflect one connotation of the original Indian terminology. The solidified duality of grasped and grasper is nothing but an invention of dualistic thought; it has that kind of character or characteristic.

Ground, Tib. gzhi: This is the first member of the formulation of ground, path, and fruition. Ground, path, and fruition is the way that the teachings of the path of oral instruction belonging to the Vajra Vehicle are presented to students. Ground refers to the basic situation as it is.

Innate, Tib. gnyug ma: This is a standard term of the higher tantras used to mean the inner situation of samsaric mind, which is its in-dwelling or innate wisdom.

Introduction and To Introduce, Tib. ngos sprad and ngos sprod pa respectively: This pair of terms is usually translated today as "pointing out" "and "to point out" but this is a mistake that has, unfortunately, become entrenched. The terms are the standard terms used in day to day life for the situation in which one person introduces another person to someone or something. They are the exact same words as our English "introduction" and "to introduce".

In the Vajra Vehicle, these terms are specifically used for the situation in which one person introduces another person to the nature of his own mind. There is a term in Tibetan for "pointing out", but that term is never used for this purpose because in this case no one points out anything. Rather, a person is introduced by another person to a part of himself that he has forgotten about.

Kagyu, Tib. bka' brgyud: There are four main schools of Buddhism in Tibet—Nyingma, Kagyu, Sakya, and Gelug. Nyingma is the oldest school dating from about 800 C.E. Kagyu and Sakya both appeared in the 12th century C.E. Each of these three schools came directly from India. The Gelug school came later and did not come directly from India but came from the other three. The Nyingma school holds the tantric teachings called Great Completion (Dzogchen); the other three schools hold the tantric teachings called Mahāmudrā. Kagyu practitioners often join Nyingma practice with their Kagyu practice and Kagyu teachers often teach both, so it is common to hear about Kagyu and Nyingma together.

Key points, Tib. gnad: Key points are those places in one's being that one works, like pressing buttons, in order to get some desired effect. For example, in meditation, there are key points of the body; by adjusting those key points, the mind is brought closer to reality and the meditation is thus assisted.

In general, this term is used in Buddhist meditation instruction but it is, in particular, part of the special vocabulary of the Great Completion teachings. Overall, the Great Completion teachings are given as a series of key points that must be attended to in order to bring forth the various realizations of the path.

Knower, Tib. ha go ba. "Knower" is a generic term for that which knows. There are many types of knower, with each having its own qualities and name, too. For example, *wisdom* is a non-dualistic knower, *mind* is the dualistic samsaric version of it, *consciousness* refers to the individual "registers" of samsaric mind, and so on. Sometimes a term is needed which simply says "that which knows" without further implication of what kind of knowing it might be; *knower* is one of a few terms of that sort.

Latency, Skt. vāsanā, Tib. bag chags: The original Sanskrit has the meaning exactly of "latency". The Tibetan term translates that inexactly with "something sitting there (Tib. chags)" within the environment of mind (Tib. bag)". Although it has become popular to translate this term into English with "habitual pattern", that is not its meaning. The term refers to a karmic seed that has been imprinted on the mindstream and is present there as a latency, ready and waiting to come into manifestation.

Luminosity or illumination, Skt. prabhāsvara, Tib. 'od gsal ba: The core of mind has two aspects: an emptiness factor and a knowing factor. The Buddha and many Indian religious teachers used "luminosity" as a metaphor for the knowing quality of the core of mind. If in English we would say "Mind has a knowing quality", the teachers of ancient India would say, "Mind has an illuminative quality; it is like a source of light which illuminates what it knows".

This term been translated as "clear light" but that is a mistake that comes from not understanding the etymology of the word. It does not refer to a light that has the quality of clearness (something that makes no sense, actually!) but to the illuminative property which is the nature of the empty mind.

Note also that in both Sanskrit and Tibetan Buddhist literature, this term is frequently abbreviated just to Skt. "vara" and Tib. "gsal ba" with no change of meaning. Unfortunately, this has been thought to be another word and it has then been translated with "clarity", when in fact it is just this term in abbreviation.

Mahamudra, Skt. mahāmudrā, Tib. phyag rgya chen po: Mahāmudrā is the name of a set of ultimate teachings on reality and also of the reality itself. This is explained at length in the book *Gampopa's Mahamudra: The Five-Part Mahamudra of the Kagyus* by Tony Duff, published by Padma Karpo Translation Committee, 2008, ISBN 978-9937-2-0607-5.

Mind, Skt. chitta, Tib. sems: There are several terms for mind in the Buddhist tradition, each with its own, specific meaning. This term is the most general term for the samsaric type of mind. It refers to the type of mind that is produced because of fundamental ignorance of enlightened mind. Whereas the wisdom of enlightened mind lacks all complexity and knows in a non-dualistic way, this mind of un-enlightenment is a very complicated apparatus that only ever knows in a dualistic way.

The Mahāmudrā and Great Completion teachings use the terms "entity of mind" and "mind's entity" to refer to what this complicated, samsaric mind is at core—the enlightened form of mind.

Post-attainment, Tib. rjes thob: See under equipoise and post-attainment.

Prajna, Skt. prajñā, Tib. shes rab: A Sanskrit term for the type of mind that makes good and precise distinctions between this and that and hence which arrives at correct understanding. It has been translated as "wisdom" but that is not correct because it is, generally speaking, a mental event belonging to dualistic mind where "wisdom" is used to refer to the non-dualistic knower of a buddha. Moreover, the main feature of prajñā is its ability to distinguish correctly between one thing and another and hence to arrive at a correct understanding.

Preserve, Tib. skyong ba: This term is important in both Mahā-mudrā and Great Completion. In general, it means to defend, protect, nurture, maintain. In the higher tantras it means to keep something just as it is, to nurture that something so that it stays and is not lost. Also, in the higher tantras, it is often used in reference to preserving the state where the state is some particular state of being. Because of this, the phrase "preserve the state" is an important instruction in the higher tantras.

Proliferation, Tib. 'phro ba: A term meaning that the dualistic mind has become active and is giving off thoughts. This is actually the same word as "elaboration" but is the intransitive sense.

Rational mind, Tib. blo: Rational mind is one of several terms for mind in Buddhist terminology. It specifically refers to a mind that judges this against that. With rare exception it is used to refer to samsaric mind, given that samsaric mind only works in the dualistic mode of comparing this versus that. Because of this, the term is mostly used in a pejorative sense to point out samsaric mind as opposed to an enlightened type of mind.

The Gelugpa tradition does have a positive meaning for this term and their documents will sometimes use it in that way;

they make the claim that a buddha has an enlightened type of this mind. That is not wrong; one could refer to the ability of a buddha's wisdom to make a distinction between this and that with the term "rational mind". However, the Kagyu and Nyingma traditions in their Mahāmudrā and Great Completion teachings reserve this term for the dualistic mind. In their teachings, it is the villain, so to speak, which needs to be removed from the practitioner's being in order to obtain enlightenment.

This term has been commonly translated simply as "mind" but that fails to identify this term properly and leaves it confused with the many other words that are also translated simply as "mind". It is not just another mind but is specifically the sort of mind that creates the situation of this and that (*ratio* in Latin) and hence, at least in the teachings of Kagyu and Nyingma, upholds the duality of saṃsāra. In that case, it is the very opposite of the essence of mind. Thus, this is a key term which should be noted and not just glossed over as "mind".

Realization, Tib. rtogs pa: Realization has a very specific meaning: it refers to correct knowledge that has been gained in such a way that the knowledge does not abate. There are two important points here. Firstly, realization is not absolute. It refers to the removal of obscurations, one at a time. Each time that a practitioner removes an obscuration, he gains a realization because of it. Therefore, there are as many levels of realization as there are obscurations. Maitreya, in the *Ornament of Manifest Realizations*, shows how the removal of the various obscurations that go with each of the three realms of samsaric existence produces realization.

Secondly, realization is stable or, as the Tibetan wording says, "unchanging". As Guru Rinpoche pointed out, "Intellectual knowledge is like a patch, it drops away; experiences on the path are temporary, they evaporate like mist; realization is unchanging".

A special usage of "realization" is found in the Essence Mahāmudrā and Great Completion teachings. There, realization is the term used to describe what happens at the moment when mindness is actually met during either introduction to or self-recognition of mindness. It is called realization because, in that glimpse, one actually directly sees the innate wisdom mind. The realization has not been stabilized but it is realization.

Rigpa, Tib. rig pa: This is the singularly most important term in the whole of Great Completion and Mahāmudrā. In particular, it is the key word of all words in the Great Completion system of the Thorough Cut. Rigpa literally means to know in the sense of "I see!" It is used at all levels of meaning from the coarsest everyday sense of knowing something to the deepest sense of knowing something as presented in the system of Thorough Cut. The system of Thorough Cut uses this term in a very special sense, though it still retains its basic meaning of "to know". To translate it as "awareness", which is common practice today, is a poor practice; there are many kinds of awareness but there is only one rigpa and besides, rigpa is substantially more than just awareness. Since this is such an important term and since it lacks an equivalent in English, I choose not to translate it.

This is the term used to indicate enlightened mind as experienced by the practitioner on the path of these practices. The term itself specifically refers to the dynamic knowing quality of mind. It absolutely does not mean a simple registering, as implied by the word "awareness" which unfortunately is often used to translate this term. There is no word in English that exactly matches it, though the idea of "seeing" or "insight on the spot" is very close. Proof of this is found in the fact that the original Sanskrit term "vidyā" is actually the root of all words in English that start with "vid" and mean "to see", for example, "video", "vision", and so on. Chogyam Trungpa Rinpoche, who was particular skilled at getting Tibetan words into English, also stated that this term rigpa really did not have a good equivalent in English, though he thought that "insight" was the closest. My own conclusion after hearing extensive teaching on it is that rigpa is best left untranslated. Note that rigpa has both noun and verb forms. To get the verb form, I use "rigpa'ing".

Samsara, Skt. saṃsāra, Tib. 'khor ba: This is the most general name for the type of existence in which sentient beings live. It refers to the fact that they continue on from one existence to another, always within the enclosure of births that are produced by ignorance and experienced as unsatisfactory. The original Sanskrit means to be constantly going about, here and there. The Tibetan term literally means "cycling", because of which it is frequently translated into English with "cyclic existence" though that is not quite the meaning of the term.

Shamatha, Skt. śhamatha, Tib. gzhi gnas: This is the name of one of the two main practices of meditation used in the Buddhist system to gain insight into reality. This practice creates a one-pointedness of mind which can then be used as a foundation for development of the insight of the other practice, vipaśhyanā. If the development of śhamatha is taken through to completion, the result is a mind that sits stably on its object without any effort and a body which is filled with ease. Altogether, this result of the practice is called "the creation of workability of body and mind".

Shine forth, shining forth, Tib. shar ba: This term means "to dawn" or "to come forth into visibility" either in the outer physical world or in the inner world of mind.

It is heavily used in texts on meditation to indicate the process of something coming forth into mind. There are other terms with this specific meaning but most of them also imply the process of dawning within a samsaric mind. "Shine forth" is special because it does not have that restricted meaning; it refers to the process of something dawning in any type of mind, un-enlightened and enlightened. It is an important term for the higher tantras of Mahāmudrā and Great Completion texts where there is a great need to refer to the simple fact of something dawning in mind especially in enlightened mind but also in un-enlightened mind.

In the Tibetan language, this term stands out and immediately conveys the meaning explained above. There are words in English like "to appear" that might seem easier to read than "shine forth", but they do not stand out and catch the attention sufficiently. Moreover, terms such as "appear" accurately translate other Tibetan terms which specifically indicate an un-enlightened context or a certain type of sensory appearance, so they do not convey the meaning of this term. There will be many times where this term's specific meaning of something occurring in any type of mind is crucial to a full understanding of the expression under consideration. For example, "shining-forth liberation" means that some content of mind, such as a thought, comes forth in either un-enlightened or enlightened mind, and that, on coming forth, is liberated there in that mind.

State, Tib. ngang: This is a key term in Mahāmudrā and Great Completion. Unfortunately it is often not translated and in so doing much meaning is lost. Alternatively, it is often translated as "within" which is incorrect. The term means a "state". A state is a certain, ongoing situation. In Buddhist meditation in general, there are various states that a practitioner has to enter and remain in as part of developing the meditation.

Temporary experience, Tib. nyams: The practice of meditation brings with it various experiences that happen simply because of doing meditation. These experiences are temporary experiences and not the final, unchanging experience, of realization.

The nature, Tib. rang bzhin: The nature is one of the three characteristics—entity, nature, and un-stopped compassionate activity—of the core of mind. Using this term emphasizes that the empty entity does have a nature. In other words, its use explicitly shows that the core of mind is not merely empty. If you ask "Well, what is that nature like?" The answer is that it is luminosity, it is wisdom.

Thorough Cut, Tib. khregs chod: The innermost level of Great Completion has two main practices, the first called Thregcho which literally translates as Thorough Cut and the second called Thogal which translates as Direct Crossing. The meaning of Thorough Cut has been misunderstood. The meaning is clearly explained in the *Illuminator Tibetan-English Dictionary*:

> Thorough Cut is a practice that slices through the solidification produced by rational mind as it grasps at a perceived object and perceiving subject. It is done in order to get to the underlying reality which is always present in the core of mind and which is called Alpha Purity in this system of teachings. For this reason, Thorough Cut is also known as Alpha Purity Thorough Cut.

The etymology of the word is explained in the Great Completion teachings either as ཁྲེགས་སུ་ཆོད་པ་ or ཁྲེགས་གི་ཆོད་པ་. In either case, the term ཆོད་པ་ is "a cut"; there are all sorts of different "cuts" and this is one of them. Then, in the case of ཁྲེགས་སུ་ཆོད་པ་, ཁྲེགས་སུ་ is an adverb modifying the verb "to cut" and has the meaning of making the cut fully, completely. It is traditionally explained with the example of slicing off a finger. A finger could be sliced with a sharp knife such that the cut was not quite complete and the cut off portion was left hanging. Alternatively, it could be sliced through in one, decisive movement such that the finger was completely and definitely severed. That kind of thorough cut is what is meant here. In the case of ཁྲེགས་གི་ཆོད་པ་, the term ཁྲེགས་གི་ is as an adverb that has the meaning of something that is doubtless, of something that is unquestionably so. A translation based on the first explanation would be "Thorough Cut" and on the second would be "Decisive Cut".

Other translations that have been put forward for this term are: "Cutting Resistance" and "Cutting Solidity". Both are grammatically incorrect. Further, the name "Cutting Resistance" is made on the basis of students expressing resistance to practice and the like, but that is not the meaning intended. Similarly, the name Cutting Solidity comes from not understanding that the term ཁྲེགས་ (khregs) has both old and new meanings; the newer meaning of "solid", "solidity" does not apply because the term Thorough Cut was put into use in the time of Padmasambhava when only the old meaning of ཁྲེགས་ was in use. The term means that the practitioner of this system cuts *decisively* through rational mind, regardless of its degree of solidity, so as to arrive directly at the essence of mind.

Upadesha, Skt. upadeśha, Tib. man ngag: See under foremost instruction.

Vipashyana, Skt. vipaśhyanā, Tib. lhag mthong: This is the Sanskrit name for one of the two main practices of meditation needed in the Buddhist system for gaining insight into reality. The other one, śhamatha, keeps the mind focussed while this one, vipaśhyanā, looks piercingly into the nature of things.

Wisdom, Skt. jñāna, Tib. ye shes: This is a fruition term that refers to the kind of mind—the kind of knower—possessed by a buddha. Sentient beings do have this kind of knower but it is covered over by a very complex apparatus for knowing, dualistic mind. If they practise the path to buddhahood, they will leave behind their obscuration and return to having this kind of knower.

The Sanskrit term has the sense of knowing in the most simple and immediate way. This sort of knowing is present at the core of every being's mind. Therefore, the Tibetans called it "the particular type of awareness which is there primordially". Because of the Tibetan wording it has often been called "primordial wisdom" in English translations, but that goes too far; it is just "wisdom" in the sense of the most fundamental knowing possible.

Wisdom does not operate in the same way as samsaric mind; it comes about in and of itself without depending on cause and effect. Therefore it is frequently referred to as "self-arising wisdom" *q.v.*

SUPPORTS FOR STUDY

I have been encouraged over the years by all of my teachers to pass on the knowledge I have accumulated in a lifetime dedicated to study and practice primarily in the Tibetan tradition of Buddhism. On the one hand, they have encouraged me to teach. On the other, they are concerned that, while many general books on Buddhism have been and are being published, there are few books that present the actual texts of the tradition. Therefore they, together with a number of major figures in the Buddhist book publishing world, have also encouraged me to translate and publish high quality translations of individual texts of the tradition.

My teachers always remark with great appreciation on the extraordinary amount of teaching that I have heard in this life. It allows for highly informed, accurate translations of a sort not usually seen. Briefly, I spent the 1970's studying, practising, then teaching the Gelugpa system at Chenrezig Institute, Australia, where I was a founding member and also the first to be ordained as a monk in the Tibetan Buddhist tradition. In 1980, I moved to the United States to study at the feet of the Vidyadhara Chogyam

Trungpa Rinpoche. I stayed in his Vajradhatu community, now called Shambhala, where I studied and practised all the Karma Kagyu, Nyingma, and Shambhala teachings being presented there. I was, at his request, a member of the Nalanda Translation Committee. After his nirvana, I moved in 1992 to Nepal, where I have been continuously involved with the study, practise, translation, and teaching of the Kagyu system and especially of the Nyingma system of Great Completion. In recent years, I have spent extended times in Tibet with the greatest living Tibetan masters of Great Completion, receiving very pure transmissions of the ultimate levels of this teaching directly in Tibetan and practising them there in retreat. In that way, I have studied and practised extensively not in one Tibetan tradition as is usually done, but in three of the four Tibetan traditions— Gelug, Kagyu, and Nyingma—and also in the Theravada tradition, too.

Padma Karpo Translation Committee (PKTC) was set up to provide a home for the translation and publication work. The committee focusses on producing books containing the best of Tibetan literature, and, especially, books that meet the needs of practitioners. At the time of writing, PKTC has published a wide range of books that, collectively, make a complete program of study for those practising Tibetan Buddhism, and especially for those interested in the higher tantras. All in all, you will find many books both free and for sale on the PKTC web-site. Most are available both as paper editions and e-books.

It would take up too much space here to present an extensive guide to our books and how they can be used as the basis for a study program. However, a guide of that sort is available on the PKTC web-site (the address is on the copyright page of this book) and we recommend that you read it to see how this book fits into the overall scheme of PKTC publications. Given that the main topic of the text in this book is Thorough Cut, some of the other PKTC publications on Thorough Cut which are important to read in conjunction with it are:

- *Flight of the Garuda* by Zhabkar
- *The Feature of the Expert, Glorious King* by Dza Patrul
- *About the Three Lines* by Dodrupchen III
- *Relics of the Dharmakaya* by Ontrul Tenpa'i Wangchuk
- *Empowerment and AtiYoga* by Tony Duff
- *Peak Doorways to Emancipation* by Shakya Shri
- *Alchemy of Accomplishment* by Dudjom Rinpoche
- *The Method of Preserving the Face of Rigpa* by Ju Mipham
- *Essential Points of Practice* by Zhechen Gyaltshab
- *Words of the Old Dog Vijay* by Zhechen Gyaltshab
- *Hinting at Dzogchen* by Tony Duff

We make a point of including, where possible, the relevant Tibetan texts in Tibetan script in our books. We also make them available in electronic editions that can be downloaded free from our web-site, as discussed below. The Tibetan text for this book is included at the back of the book and is available for download from the PKTC web-site.

Electronic Resources

PKTC has developed a complete range of electronic tools to facilitate the study and translation of Tibetan texts. For many years now, this software has been a prime resource for Tibetan Buddhist centres throughout the world, including in Tibet itself. It is available through the PKTC web-site.

The wordprocessor TibetDoc has the only complete set of tools for creating, correcting, and formatting Tibetan text according to the norms of the Tibetan language. It can also be used to make texts with mixed Tibetan and English or other languages. Extremely high quality Tibetan fonts, based on the forms of Tibetan calligraphy learned from old masters from pre-Communist Chinese Tibet, are also available. Because of their excellence, these typefaces have achieved a legendary status amongst Tibetans.

TibetDoc is used to prepare electronic editions of Tibetan texts in the PKTC text input office in Asia. Tibetan texts are often corrupt, so the input texts are carefully corrected prior to distribution. After that, they are made available through the PKTC web-site. These electronic texts are not careless productions like so many of the Tibetan texts found on the web, but are highly reliable editions useful to non-scholars and scholars alike. Some of the larger collections of these texts are for purchase, but most are available for free download.

The electronic texts can be read, searched, and even made into an electronic library using either TibetDoc or our other software, TibetD Reader. Like TibetDoc, TibetD Reader is advanced software with many capabilities made specifically to meet the needs of reading and researching Tibetan texts. PKTC software is for purchase but we make a free version of TibetD Reader available for free download on the PKTC web-site.

A key feature of TibetDoc and Tibet Reader is that Tibetan terms in texts can be looked up on the spot using PKTC's electronic dictionaries. PKTC also has several electronic dictionaries—some Tibetan-Tibetan and some Tibetan-English—and a number of other reference works. The *Illuminator Tibetan-English Dictionary* is renowned for its completeness and accuracy.

This combination of software, texts, reference works, and dictionaries that work together seamlessly has become famous over the years. It has been the basis of many, large publishing projects within the Tibetan Buddhist community around the world for over thirty years and is popular amongst all those needing to work with Tibetan language or deepen their understanding of Buddhism through Tibetan texts.

TIBETAN TEXT

༄༅། །རྟོགས་ལྡན་རྒྱན་པོ་རྣམས་ཀྱི་ལུགས་སེམས་དོ་མཛུབ་ཚུགས་
ཀྱི་གདམས་པ་སྨུན་སེལ་སྒྲོན་མེ་བཞུགས་སོ།།

༄༅། །བླ་མ་དང་འཇམ་དཔལ་ཡེ་ཤེས་སེམས་དཔའ་ལ་ཕྱག་འཚལ་
ལོ། །ཐོས་བསམ་སྒོམ་བ་རྒྱུ་ཆེན་མི་དགོས་པར། །ཨན་ངག་ལུགས་ཀྱིས་
སེམས་དོ་སྒོམ་བ་ཡི། །ཁྱོང་སྤྱགས་ཕལ་མོ་ཆེ་ཞིག་ཚོགས་ཆུང་དུས། །
རིག་འཛིན་ས་ལ་གཤེགས་ཏེ་ལམ་ཟབ་མཐུ། །དེ་ཡང་རང་གི་སེམས་འདི་
རང་བབས་སུ་ཅི་ཡང་མི་བསམ་པར་བཞག་ནས་དེ་ཡི་ངང་དུ་དྲན་པའི་རྒྱུན་
བསྐྱང་བ་དེ་ཡི་ཚེ། །བདང་སྐྱོམས་ལྱང་མ་བསྐྱན་གྱི་ཤེས་པ་སྨུན་ནེ་ཐོམ་མེ་བ་
ཞིག་འབྱུང་། །དེ་ལ་འདི་ཤེས་དེ་ཤེས་ཀྱི་ལྷག་མཐོང་གང་ཡང་མ་སྐྱེས་པའི་ཚོ་
ན། །དེའི་ཆ་ནས་བླ་མ་དག་གིས་མ་རིག་པར་མིང་འདོགས་པར་འདུག །
དེ་ལ་འདི་འདུ་འདེ་ཡིན་གྱི་ངོས་བཟུང་སྐྱམས་ཤེས་པའི་ཆ་ནས་ལྱང་མ་བསྐྱན་ཞེས་
མིང་བཏགས། །ཅི་ལ་གནས་དང་ཅི་བསམ་པ་སྐྱར་མེད་པས་ཐ་མལ་བཏང་
སྐྱོམས་ཞེས་བཏགས་ཏེ། །ཡིན་ནི་ཀུན་གཞིའི་ངང་དུ་ཐ་མལ་རང་གར་བསྐྱང་

41

པ་ཡིན། བཞག་ཐབས་དེ་འདྲ་བ་ལ་བརྟེན་ནས་མི་རྟོག་ཡེ་ཤེས་བསྐྱེད་དགོས་

གྱུང་། རང་རོ་རིག་པའི་ཡེ་ཤེས་མ་ཤར་བ་དེ་འདྲ་སྟོང་གི་དངོས་གཞི་མ་ཡིན་

ཏེ། ཀུན་སློང་ལས། ཅི་ཡང་དྲན་མེད་ཐོམ་མེ་བཿ དེ་ཀ་མ་རིག་

འཁྲུལ་པའི་རྒྱུཿ ཞེས་གསུངས་པ་བཞིན་ནོ། །དེ་ལྟར་ཅི་ཡང་མ་དྲན་མ་

འགྱུས་པའི་ཤེས་པ་ཐོམ་མེ་བ་དེ་འདྲ་སེམས་ཀྱིས་སྐྱོང་བས་ན། དེ་འདྲའི་དོན་

ཤེས་མཁན་དང་མི་བསམ་པར་འདུག་མཁན་ཁོ་རང་ལ་བབས་ཀྱིས་བལྟས་པས།

འགྱུ་དྲན་བྲལ་བའི་རིག་པ་ཕྱི་ནང་མེད་པར་ཟང་ཐལ་ལེ་བ་ནས་མཁན་དྲངས་པ་

ལྟ་བུ། སྒྱུང་བུ་སྐྱོང་བྱེད་གཉིས་མེད་གྱུང་རང་གི་རང་བཞིན་རང་གིས་ཁོ་ཐག

ཆོད་ནས་འདི་ལས་གཞན་ཅི་ཡང་མི་འདུག་སྣམ་པ་བྱུང་ན། དེ་ལ་བསམ་

བཟོད་ཀྱིས་འདི་འདྲ་ཞེས་སྨྲ་མེད་པས་མཐའ་བྲལ་དང་བཟོད་བྲལ་དང་གཅུག

མའི་འོད་གསལ་དང་། རིག་པ་ཞེས་བཏགས་ཆོག་སྟེ། རང་རོ་འཕོད་

པའི་ཡེ་ཤེས་ཤར་བས་དགུ་ཐོམ་མེ་བའི་མུན་པ་དྲངས་ཏེ་ནམ་ལངས་པས་ཕྱིམ་

ནང་མཐོང་བ་ལྟར་རང་གི་སེམས་ཀྱི་ཆོས་ཉིད་ལ་ངེས་ཤེས་སྐྱེས་པས་སོ། །

འདི་ལ་མ་རིག་སྨྲོ་ངའི་སྒྲུབས་འཕྱེད་པའི་མན་ངག་ཅེས་བྱའོ། །དེ་ལྟར་

རྟོགས་ཚེ་ཆོས་ཉིད་དེ་ལྟ་བུའི་རང་བཞིན་བབ་ཀྱིས་ཡེ་ནས་གནས་པས་རྒྱུ་རྐྱེན་

གྱིས་འདུས་མ་བྱས་པ་དང་། དུས་གསུམ་འཕོ་འགྱུར་མེད་པ་ཡིན་པར་ཤེས་

ཤིང་། དེ་ལས་གཞན་དུ་གྱུར་པའི་སེམས་ཞེས་བྱ་བ་རྫལ་ཚམ་ཡང་ཡོད་པར་

མི་དམིགས་སོ། །སྤུ་མ་མུན་ཐོམ་མེ་བ་དེ་ལ་བཟོད་དུ་མེད་གྱུང་། ཅི་ཡང་

བཟོད་མ་ཤེས་པས་ཁོ་ཐག་མ་ཆོད་པ་ཡིན་ལ། རིག་རོ་ལ་བཟོད་དུ་མེད་གྱུང

བཟོད་མེད་ཀྱི་དོན་ལ་ཐེ་ཚོམ་མེད་པའི་ཁོ་ཐག་ཆོད་པས། སྨིག་མེད་དང་མིག

སྤྲུན་ལྟར་འདི་གཉིས་ཀྱི་བཟོད་དུ་མེད་ཆུལ་ཁྱད་ཆེ་བས། ཀུན་གཞི་དང་ཆོས་

སྐུའི་དབྱེ་བ་ཡང་འདིར་གནད་འདུས་སོ། །དེས་ན་ཐ་མལ་གྱི་ཤེས་པ་ཞེས་པ

དང་། ཡིད་ལ་མི་བྱེད་པ་དང་། བརྗོད་བྲལ་སོགས་ལ་ཡང་དག་ཡིན་མིན་
གཉིས་ཡོད་པས་སྐྱ་མཐུན་རྟེན་འཕགས་ཀྱི་གནད་ངེས་པར་བྱུས་ན་ཟབ་མོའི་ཚོས་
ཀྱི་དགོངས་རྣམས་རྟེད་པར་འགྱུར་རོ། །སེམས་ཉིད་དང་དུ་རང་བབ་བཞག་
ཚོ་ཁ་ཅིག་གིས་གསལ་ཙམ་རིག་ཙམ་སྐྱོང་ཆྱུར་བྱུས་ཏེ་ཡིད་ཤེས་ཀྱིས་གསལ་
ལོ་སྐྱམ་པའི་དང་དུ་འཛིག །ཁ་ཅིག་གིས་སྐྱོང་ཚམ་མེ་བ་ཤེས་པ་སྐྱོང་སོང་བ་
ཀླུ་བུ་ལ་སེམས་འཛིན་ཀྱང་། འདི་གཉིས་ཀ་ཡིད་ཤེས་ཀྱི་ཆ་གཟུང་འཛིན་གྱི་
རྣམས་ལ་ཞེན་པ་ཚམ་ཡིན་པས། དེའི་ཚེ་གསལ་བ་དང་གསལ་བར་འཛིན་
མཁན། སྐྱོང་པ་དང་སྐྱོང་པར་འཛིན་མཁན་གྱི་ཤེས་པ་དྲན་འཛིན་གྱི་རྒྱུད་བྱེད་
དེ་བ་དེའི་བབ་ལ་བལྟས་པས། གཟུང་འཛིན་དུ་ཞེན་པའི་རྣམ་ཤེས་ཀྱི་རྟེན་ཕྱུར་
ཕྱུངས་ཏེ་རྟེན་ནེ་ཡེ་རེ་བ་གསལ་སྐྱོང་མཐའ་དབུས་དང་བྲལ་བའི་རང་བབ་ཁོ་
ཐག་ཆོད་དེ་དྲངས་མེང་དེ་བ་བྱུང་ན་དེ་ལ་རིག་དོ་ཞེས་མིང་འདོགས་ཏེ། །
འཛིན་པ་ཅན་གྱི་རྣམས་ཀྱི་ཤུན་པ་དང་བྲལ་བའི་རིག་པ་ཡེ་ཤེས་རྟེན་པར་ཤར་བ་
ཡིན་ནོ། །འདི་ལ་སྒྱིད་པའི་དྲ་བ་གཙོད་པའི་མན་ངག་ཅེས་བྱའོ། །དེ་
བཞིན་དུ་ཡིད་དཔྱོད་རྣམས་ཀྱི་སྨུན་པ་སྣ་ཚོགས་དང་བྲལ་བའི་རིག་པ་འབྱས་སྟེའུ་
ཀླུ་བུ་ཚོས་ཉིད་ཀྱི་རང་བབ་རང་གསལ་གྱི་སྣོ་ནས་དོས་ཟིན་པར་བྱའོ། །རིག་
པའི་བབ་དོ་ཤེས་པ་ཚམ་གྱིས་མི་ཆོག་པར་དེ་གའི་དང་དུ་གོམས་པའི་གནས་ཚ་
བརྟན་དགོས་པས། ཤེས་པ་རང་བབ་བཞག་པའི་དྲུན་རྒྱུ་མ་ཡེངས་པར་སྐྱོང་
བ་གལ་ཆེ། དེ་ལྟར་སྐྱོང་དུས་རེས་ཅེ་ཡིན་མེད་པའི་མི་རྟོག་རྨུན་པོ། རེས་
ཀླུག་མཐོང་གི་དྲངས་ཆ་ཐོན་པའི་མི་རྟོག་ཟང་ཐལ། རེས་བདེ་རྣམས་ཞེན་པ་
ཅན། རེས་བདེ་རྣམས་ཞེན་མེད། རེས་སྣ་ཚོགས་གསལ་རྣམས་འཛིན་པ་
ཅན། རེས་དྲངས་གསལ་རྣོག་མེད་འཛིན་བྲལ། རེས་རྡུབ་རྣམས་མི་སྐྲག་
པ། རེས་འཛམ་རྣམས་ཡིད་འོང་། རེས་རྣམ་རྟོག་ཆེས་འཚུབ་ཆེ་བའི་ཕྱིར་

འབྱུངས་ནས་སྐོམ་སྟོར་བ། རེས་འཐིབས་དངས་མི་ཕྱེད་པས་རྟོག་པ་ཅན་
སོགས། ཐིག་མེད་ནས་གོམས་པའི་རྣམ་རྟོག་དང་ལས་རླུང་གི་ཐ་རྩབས་སླ་
ཚོགས་ངེས་པ་དང་ཚད་བཟུང་མེད་པར་འབྱུང་བ་ནི། ལམ་རིང་པོར་ཞུགས་
པས་བདེ་གཟར་སྟུ་ཚོགས་ཀྱི་གནས་མཐོང་བ་དང་འདྲ་བས་གང་ཤར་ཆེད་འཛིན་
མེད་པར་རང་ལམ་བསྒུང། ལྷག་པར་མ་གོམས་པའི་དུས་ན་རྣམ་རྟོག་སླ་
ཚོགས་མེ་ལྕེར་འབར་བ་གཡོ་བའི་ཉམས་ཀྱི་དུས་སུ་དེས་མ་སྒུན་པར་བྱུས་ཏེ།
སྐོམ་སྟོད་རན་པོས་རྒྱུན་མ་བཏང་བར་བསྒུང་བས་ཐོབ་པ་སོགས་ཉམས་ཕྱི་མ་
དག་རིམ་བཞིན་འབྱུང་རོ། །འདི་དུས་སྟྱེར་རིག་པ་དང་མ་རིག་པ། །ཀུན་
གཞི་དང་ཚེས་སྨ། རྣམ་ཤེས་དང་། ཡེ་ཤེས་ཀྱི་ཁྱད་པར་བླ་མའི་མན་ངག་
གིས་ཉམས་སྐྱོང་གི་སྟེང་ནས་ཕོ་འཕྲོད་པ་གཏེང་དུ་བྱུས་ནས། སྐྱོང་དུས་རྒྱུ་
མ་བསྒུལ་ན་དངས་པ་ལྟར། རྣམ་ཤེས་རང་སར་བཞག་པས་དེའི་ཚོས་ཉིད་ཡེ་
ཤེས་རང་བྱུང་དུ་གསལ་བའི་མན་དག་གཙོ་བོར་བྱ་དགོས་ཀྱི། བདག་གི་
སྐོམ་རྒྱ་འདི་རྣམ་ཤེས་སམ་ཡེ་ཤེས་གང་ཡིན་ཞེས་སྤྲུང་བྱུང་གི་དཔྱད་ར་དང་དཔེ་
ཚའི་གོ་རྟོག་གི་འདུ་འཕྲོ་སྒྱུལ་བར་མི་བྱ་སྟེ། དེས་ཞེ་ལྷག་གཉིས་ཀ་ཅུང་ཟད་
སྒྲིབ་པར་འགྱུར་རོ། །རང་བབ་འཛིག་པའི་དུན་པའི་རྒྱུན་བརྟན་པའི་ཞི་གནས་
ཀྱི་གོམས་ཆ་དང་། རང་རོ་རང་གསལ་དུ་ཤེས་པའི་ལྷག་མཐོང་རང་ཤུགས་
ཀྱིས་འཐྱེལ་བའི་ཆུལ་དུ་གོམས་པ་བརྟན་པོར་སོང་བ་ན། རང་བབ་ཡེ་གནས་
དང་། རང་བཞིན་འོད་གསལ་གྱི་ཞི་ལྷག་ཡེ་ནས་དབྱེར་མེད་པ་རང་བྱུང་གི་
ཡེ་ཤེས་རྟོགས་པ་ཆེན་པོའི་དགོངས་པ་འཆར་བར་འགྱུར་རོ། །འདི་ནི་མཁའ་
ལྟར་མཉམ་པ་ཉིད་ལ་གནས་པའི་མན་དག་གོ །དེ་ལྟར་ཡང་དཔལ་ས་ར་
ཧས། བསམ་དང་བསམ་བྱ་རབ་ཏུ་སྤངས་ནས་སུ། །བསམ་མེད་བྱ་རྒྱུང་
ཚུལ་དུ་གནས་བྱ་ཞིང་། །ཞེས་བཞག་ཐབས་དང་། བླ་མའི་ལུང་ལ

བསྐྱིལ་སྟེ་རབ་འབད་ན། །ཞེས་རིག་པ་ངོ་སྤྲུད་པའི་མན་ངག་དང་ལྟུན་པར་
བྱས་ན། །ལྟུན་ཚིག་སྨྲས་པ་འབྱུང་བར་བྱེ་ཚོམ་མེད། །ཅེས་གདོད་ནས་
རང་གི་སེམས་དང་ལྟུན་ཚིག་སྨྲས་པ་སེམས་ཀྱི་ཚོས་ཉིད་རིག་པ་རང་བྱུང་གི་ཡེ་
ཤེས་འབྱུང་སྟེ། །དེ་ནི་ཚོས་ཀུན་གྱི་ཚོས་ཉིད་དང་ཐ་དད་མེད་པ་གཤུག་མ་དོན་
གྱི་འོད་གསལ་གྱང་ཡིན་ནོ། །དེས་ན་རང་བབ་བཞག་པ་དང་། རང་ངོ་
ཤེས་པའི་རིག་པའམ་སེམས་ཀྱི་ངོ་བོའམ་ཚོས་ཉིད་སྐྱོང་ཚུལ་འདི་གནད་བཅུ་
གཅིག་འདུས་ཀྱི་མན་ངག་ཡིན། །རྒྱུན་དུ་སྐྱོང་རྒྱུང་དེ་ཡིན། །བོགས་པའི་
ཚོད་ནི་མཆོན་མེའི་འོད་གསལ་གྱིས་འཛིན། །ཡང་དག་པའི་ལམ་ཡིན་པའི་
རྟགས་ནི་དང་པ་དང་སྟེང་རྗེ་ཤེས་རབ་སོགས་རང་ཤུགས་ཀྱིས་འཕེལ་བས་
རྟོགས། །བདེ་ཞིང་ཚེགས་ཆུང་བ་ནི་རང་གི་ཉམས་སུ་མྱོང་བས་ཤེས། །
ཟབ་ཚིང་མྱུར་བ་ནི་ཤིན་ཏུ་འབད་རྩོལ་ཆེན་པོས་བསྒྲུབ་པའི་ལམ་གཞན་ལ་ལྟགས་
པ་རྣམས་དང་རྟོགས་ཚད་བསྡུན་པས་ངེས་པ་ཡིན་ནོ། །རང་སེམས་འོད་
གསལ་བསྐྱིལ་པས་འབྲས་བུ་ཐོབ་རྒྱུའང་དེའི་སྟེང་གི་རྣམ་རྟོག་དང་དེའི་བག་
ཆགས་ཀྱི་སྒྲིབ་པ་རང་སངས་ཚོ། །མཐྲེན་གཉིས་ཚུལ་མེད་དུ་རྒྱས་ནས་གདོད་
མའི་གཏན་སྲིད་ཟིན་ཏེ་སྐུ་གསུམ་ལྟུན་གྱིས་གྲུབ་པ་ཡིན་ནོ། །ཟབ་པོ། གུ་
ཧྱཿ ས་མ་ཡཿ རབ་ཚོས་མེ་ཏ་ཟྲ་ར་ཚོས་༡༢་ལ་ཐོས་བསམ་ལ་ཆེར་མི་
བཙོན་ཀྱང་སེམས་ངོའི་རྣམས་ཡེན་འདོད་པའི་གྲོང་སྤྱགས་པ་སོགས་ཀྱི་ཆེད་དུ།
རྟོགས་ལྟུན་རྒྱན་པོ་ཐལ་གྱི་རྣམས་སྐྱོང་དམར་ཁྲིད་ཀྱི་ཚོས་སྐྱད་གོ་བདེ་དང་
བསྡུན་པའི་གདམས་པ་ཟབ་མོ་མི་ཐམ་འཛམ་དཔལ་རྡོ་རྗེས་བཀོད་པ་
དགོའོ། །མངྐ་ལཾ།། ॥

INDEX

47